Reflections of Swansea

South Wales
Evening Post

Reflections of Swansea

by David Roberts

breedon **books**
PUBLISHING

First published in Great Britain in 2001 by
The Breedon Books Publishing Company Limited
Breedon House, 3 The Parker Centre, Derby, DE21 4SZ.

ISBN 1 85983 264 4

Printed and bound by Butler & Tanner Ltd, Frome, Somerset
Jacket printing by GreenShires Ltd, Leicester

Contents

Foreword 7

Swansea, Old and New 8

Changing Places 9

Friendly Faces 49

Entertaining Ways 69

Days Of Destruction 77

Unforgettable Moments 87

On Parade 104

District Diary 113

Early Learning 132

Beside The Seaside 154

Moving Memories 167

Working Wonders 181

Team Spirit 199

An Appreciation

This book would not have been possible without the valued assistance of readers of the *South Wales Evening Post* and the many residents of Swansea who submitted their own images of days gone by.
Particular thanks are due to:

Ray Stock
David Beynon
Alwyn Hughes
Peter Seaward
Nanci Shapton
Hazel Rees
Cyril Ogborn
Judith Ruscitto
Steve Powell
Colin Miller and Cheryl Roberts.

Foreword

SWANSEA is set to undergo one of the most significant periods of planned change in its history. So the time has never been more apt to record what has gone before. Change of any degree always leaves behind memories, but these can be fragile and fade as years pass. Reflections of Swansea follows three successful companion volumes in forming a unique album of images of the city and surrounding areas. Its pictures will breathe new life into many moments from the past. People, places and events that have all played a part in the emergence of Swansea as Wales's seaside city are all included. Some scenes will be familiar, others not so. Mixed together they provide fascinating proof that though it values tradition the city is not afraid to move with the times. The South Wales Evening Post is delighted to be involved with the author, and all those who have helped in bringing such a collection together as a further salute to the proud people of Swansea. It will be enjoyed by all who turn its pages.

George Edwards
Editor
South Wales Evening Post

Swansea, Old and New

Old Swansea town couldn't have been more different from the vibrant, modern city of the 21st century. Its tightly-knit, narrow, winding streets, bursting with countless cosy shops, and attractive buildings can never be compared with the wide, straight roads and sprawling look-alike stores that took their place. Function rather than beauty appears to have been the watchword of most of the modern architecture.

This change was no gradual metamorphosis. Nor one created from choice. It was the result of the catastrophic Three Nights' Blitz of February 1941. At a stroke that wartime event erased centuries of Swansea's heritage. With the slate wiped clean it was inevitable that the planner's vogue would be for buildings that were light, airy and, at the time, futuristic.

Many street names vanished, new ones were born. Gone were Temple Street, Waterloo Street and Goat Street. Instead came names like Princess Way, The Kingsway and Whitewalls. The destruction had been so great it took more than two decades to remodel the town. And though not all the changes were welcomed it was a place its people could be proud of again.

It was perhaps appropriate that the labours of those who bravely resurrected Swansea from the ashes of war should be rewarded when, in 1969, it achieved city status.

Since then, change has been more subtle, but it is always happening. The Swansea of today is the result of 900 years of development. The images of people and places in this book link three of those centuries to reflect that.

David Roberts
2001

Changing Places

The Salisbury Club, Wind Street, late 1890s.

Oxford Street, looking westwards from the town centre, early 1900s.

The birthplace of renowned architect Beau Nash, Caer Street, Swansea, in use as a clothiers, in the early 1900s.

Looking up High Street, 1902.

Looking down High Street, with the Palace Theatre on the left, 1904.

All that remained of Swansea Market after it was gutted by fire on the night of May 26, 1905.

Walter Road, looking towards the centre of town, 1905.

High Street, looking up, towards the railway station, 1905.

Oxford Street, with the Empire Theatre, on the right, 1906.

Oxford Street, looking east, 1906.

The junction of Mount Pleasant and De La Beche Street, 1906.

High Street, near its junction with Kings Lane, 1907.

The millinery and drapery store of B Tudor Davies, 17 & 18 Gors Lane, 1907.

Castle Street, looking towards High Street, 1909.

King Edward Road, 1909.

Castle Street, 1909. When this picture was taken demolition work was about to start to widen the street.

College Street, 1910.

Walter Road, 1910.

High Street, 1911.

The harbour offices, at the corner of Adelaide Street and Somerset Place, 1912.

Dumbarton House School, Uplands, 1913.

High Street, near the railway station, 1916.

Construction of the arches carrying the railway across the Strand into and out of Swansea, 1924.

Glanmor School and above, the Training College, about 1934.

The Technical College, Mount Pleasant, 1932.

An aerial view of the mouth of the River Tawe, mid-1930s.

The Plaza cinema, mid-1930s.

Temple Street, looking down into Oxford Street, late 1930s. It was destroyed in the wartime blitz of February, 1941.

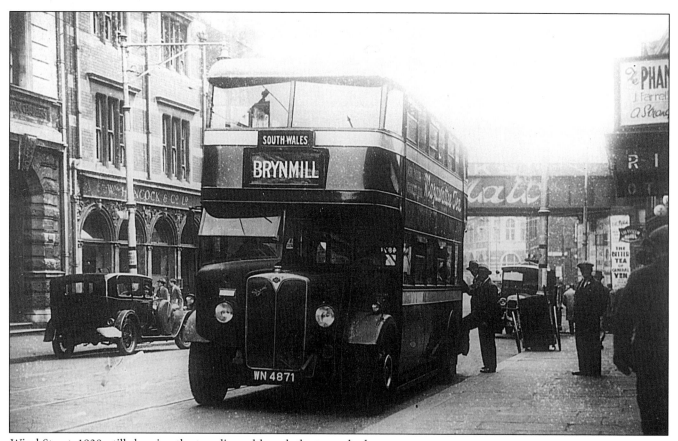

Wind Street, 1938, still showing the tramlines although the trams had gone.

The Victoria Park fountain and behind, Swansea Guildhall, 1939.

Castle Bailey Street, June 1941.

How Swansea looked from the air in 1950 as it began to rebuild after the wartime blitz of 1941.

Heathfield Street, old Swansea's equivalent to London's Harley Street, 1946.

Wind Street, 1950. Before long Swan buses would vanish forever from the old town's streets.

Orchard Street, early 1950s.

A wintry Castle Gardens, with Princess Way in the foreground, 1953.

St Mary's Church surrounded by scaffolding in the mid-1950s during its rebuilding after bomb and fire damage during World War Two.

The roundabout at the eastern end of The Kingsway, mid-1950s.

Castle Gardens, mid-1950s.

Castle Gardens and Castle Bailey Street, June 1956.

Princess Way, 1956.

High Street, 1957.

The Grand Hotel, opposite High Street Railway Station, 1958.

High Street, 1958. Probably pictured on a quiet Sunday.

St Mary Street, 1958. The steel framework became the city's popular C&A fashion store.

Singleton Street, 1959.

Oxford Street, 1959.

The Guildhall, viewed from Victoria Gardens, 1959.

High Street, looking towards the Palace Theatre, on the right, 1960.

A 1960s view of the area now occupied by The Quadrant shopping centre.

Castle Street, early 1960s.

Oxford Street, and the market entrance, January 1962.

St Helen's Road, 1962.

The Cuba railway bridge across the main eastern traffic route into Swansea, early 1962.

Lower Oxford Street, with Oxford Street Junior School, on the right, 1963.

Building work in progress on J.T. Morgan's new warehouse, Belle Vue Way, early 1960s.

The famous bear at the No. 10, mid-1960s.

The balcony bar at the No. 10, mid-1960s.

The No. 10 public house, Union Street mid-1960s.

The fountain at Castle Gardens, mid-1960s. It can now be found in the botanical gardens at Singleton Park.

Quay Parade, the new main eastern traffic artery with Weaver's flour mill on the left, August 1965.

Mansel Street, 1966.

The Kingsway, 1968.

A night-time view of Caer Street, Princess Way and Castle Gardens, 1968.

Mount Pleasant, 1968.

The queue stretched right along Nelson Street when the Walkaround store held a sale of fire-damaged goods, late-1960s.

Swansea Guildhall, late-1960s.

An aerial view of central Swansea, 1971. The Kingsway multi-storey car park and the roof of the Odeon cinema can clearly be seen on the right of the picture.

Western Street, flooded for the second time in five days, 1971.

St Helen's Road, 1972.

Work starts to turn the roundabout at the junction of The Kingsway and Princess Way into a pedestrian underpass, October 1972.

Alexandra Road, 1974.

Foundation work under way on the Quadrant Shopping Centre, 1974. Before long this view of Swansea market's arched roof would be lost for good.

Princess Way, 1975.

A bird's-eye view of Swansea, looking towards the River Tawe, 1975.

St Helen's Road, 1976.

An unusual late-1970s Swansea panorama. Vetch Field, home of Swansea City Football Club, is in the centre.

Swansea Castle is overshadowed by the city's BT tower, 1976.

Unusually clear of traffic, this was Mumbles Road, Blackpill, near the entrance to Singleton Park after a heavy snowfall early in 1982.

Work under way on the St David's multi-storey car park, early 1980s.

Friendly Faces

Nearly all the villagers at Sketty gathered together for this 1897 picture.

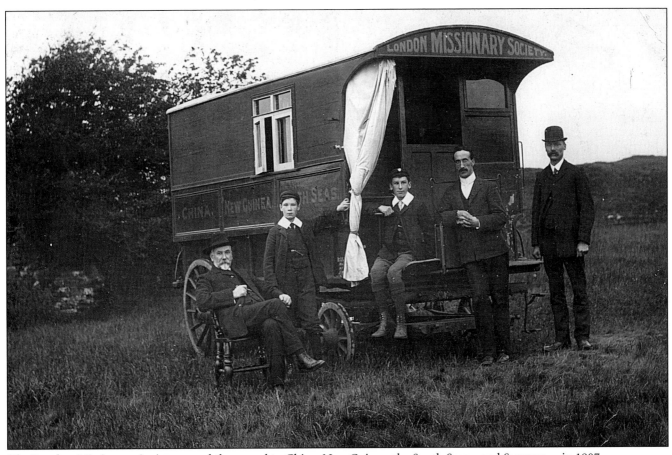

The London Missionary Society spread the gospel to China, New Guinea, the South Seas – and Swansea – in 1907…

…And this was the crowd that assembled to hear the words of the London Missionary Society.

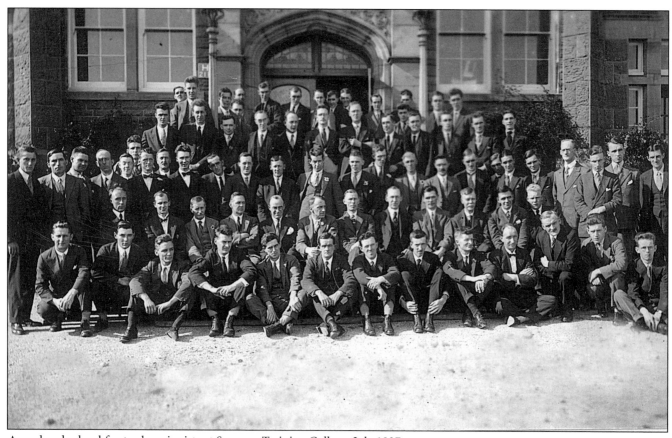

A weekend school for trade unionists at Swansea Training College, July 1927.

St Stephen's Church men's club, 1929. The man on the right is the father of the late Sir Harry Secombe.

Staff of James Brothers, milliners and drapers, of High Street, on their annual outing, 1930.

A Swansea family pauses for a rest while out for a Sunday walk to Brynmill Park, early 1930s.

Friends and neighbours from Brynhyfryd, off on a day trip, early 1930s.

Members of Swansea Boys' Club cheering their president, chief constable of the town's police force, Mr F.J. May at their New Year party, 1937.

A Christmas party at Swansea Boys' Club in Salubrious Passage, 1937.

Time for study at Swansea Boys' Club, 1937.

Some of those from North Hill Road and Hill Street, who went on the North Hill Church Whitsun outing to Dunvant Park, May 1938.

Neighbours and friends gather in Neath Road, Plasmarl, for a presentation to a serviceman off to fight the war, 1941.

Civic leaders attend a gathering of Swansea Quakers, 1942.

Terrace Road Men's Guild all set for a day out, 1948.

Friends and neighbours of Caemawr, Clydach, on a trip to Cheltenham, April 16, 1949.

Swansea market stallholders enjoy themselves on their annual outing, 1949.

Members of the Swansea branch of the National Federation of Master Painters and Decorators of England and Wales at their annual dinner and dance, 1950.

Regulars of the Maltsters public house, Cwmbwrla, outside R.J. Shaddick's TV and radio shop, Waun Wen before setting off on a day trip, early 1950s.

Members of the congregation of Calfaria Chapel, Morriston, all set for a day out, 1950.

Cwm Level Road, Landore was the scene of a fancy dress football competition to celebrate the coronation of Queen Elizabeth II, in June 1953. The men from Landeg Street, Plasmarl, dressed as women for the event…

…And their wives dressed in football kit.

Members and guests of Swansea Central Cycling Club at its 1952 dinner dance.

Some of the staff of High Street drapers and milliners, James Brothers, on a coach trip, 1954.

Children from Eastmoor Nursery, Clyne Common, take it in turns to give one another cart rides, 1954.

Trophy winners at a dancing competition held at The Casino, Mumbles, March 1956.

Former pupils of Dynevor School at an old Dyvorians dinner at the Mackworth Hotel, High Street, 1956.

Waiting for the film fun to begin at Morriston Scout's Christmas party, 1957.

David Holder and Janice Williams, winners of the Edward Newton School of Dancing annual competition, surrounded by fellow competitors, 1957.

Staff of the Swansea branch of Burtons men's outfitters, and their guests at the stores annual dinner and dance, held at The Langland Court Hotel, 1959.

Mr Sidney Heath with staff of his Caer Street store's Maids department – girls and school outfitting – at the store's Christmas party, early 1960s.

A group of friends at Mumbles Rugby Club, 1960s.

Members of the 44th Sketty Scout troop prepare for a cycling trip to the Isle of Wight, 1962.

Staff of outfitters Sidney Heath before setting off on their annual outing to Wookey Hole, 1963.

Sidney Heath staff travelled to Longleat for their summer outing, in June 1967.

Staff of Burtons outfitters with guests at their annual dinner and dance, 1968.

Officials and guests at Townhill and Mayhill Horticultural Society's show, August 24, 1968.

Children fish in the canal at Morriston, 1968.

Patients and nurses pose for the cameraman outside one of the male wards at Morriston hospital, 1969.

Employees of Mettoy in the works canteen, on April 3, 1973, for the presentation of the factory's first 25 year long-service awards. Some of the recipients are pictured with managers and colleagues.

Workers of Viscose at a staff presentation, late 1970s.

Entertaining Ways

The Eureka Party, formed by residents of Plasmarl and Landore, 1925.

These young ladies from Sketty were all dressed up for a gang show, early 1930s.

The New Broadways, a popular Swansea band, late 1930s.

The cast of a pantomime performed at the Bryn Hall, Brynhyfryd, by members of Manselton Congregational Chapel Band of Hope, 1947.

Libanus Chapel Dramatic Society, 1948.

Townhill Merry Boys minstrel-style band, 1950s.

A section of the Townhill Merry Boys concert party, 1950s.

Penclawdd Mixed Choir pictured before leaving for the Llangollen International Eisteddfod, 1951.

Brynmill Senior Girls School pupils who took part in a Festival of Britain pageant at the Brangwyn Hall, May 1951.

Young members of the audience meet the cast of a pantomime held at the Empire Theatre, early 1950s.

Members of St Augustine's Amateur Dramatic Society during a production at St Gabriel's Church Hall, Bryn Road, 1952.

The Magnet Club Male Voice Choir, 1954. The Magnet was the staff club for employees of South Wales Transport.

Some of those who took part in the Swansea schools singing festival at the Brangwyn Hall, June 28, 1956. They performed Handel's Messiah.

The cast of a Sketty Baptist Church concert, 1960.

Members of Townhill Ranger Guides with some of the younger members of the cast of a show they produced, June 1969.

The cast of Broadway School's 1976 Nativity play.

The choir of St Michael's and All Angels' Church, Manselton, 1971.

Days of Destruction

THE Three Nights' Blitz suffered by Swansea during World War Two is the most significant event in the city's history. The effects of the aerial bombardment which claimed the lives of 230 of its citizens on February 19, 20 and 21, 1941, are still being felt more than 60 years later. During the relentless attacks the heart of the old town was consumed by a raging firestorm. When it had burned itself out life for the survivors would never be the same. Rebuilding was a task that took decades. The pictures here help provide some indication of the scale of the destruction. Most were taken in the days and months after the event..

Firefighters damp down the ruins of the Ben Evans department store in Castle Bailey Street after the third night of the Blitz.

Hodges' Corner, at the junction of High Street and College Street.

The remains of the Adelaide Hotel, Adelaide Street. The South Wales Evening Post offices were later built on the site.

Gower Street, looking westwards towards its junction with Union Street. The South Wales Furnishers store and Music Hall Hotel had stood on the corner until the bombers reduced them to rubble.

Caer Street, almost obliterated by the bombs.

When daylight broke after the third night of the bombings, buildings had been flattened and streets in the centre of the town were blocked by rubble.

Looking down Oxford Street, from the upper windows of the old South Wales Evening Post Offices, Castle Bailey Street.

The remains of the Plough Hotel, Portland Street, looking towards the market entrance.

All that remained of Swansea Grammar School.

Rubble and twisted girders were all that remained of Pell Street, alongside the modern day Post Office in The Kingsway.

The centre of the town was a scene of total devastation as this picture of the former David Evans department store in Goat Street shows.

The ferocity of the fires started by the incendiary bombs gutted acres of buildings and left their girder framework just a tangled web of twisted metal. This picture was taken looking down Portland Street towards Park Street.

Tired and weary after the toil and struggle to clear the blocked streets of rubble and restore order to the chaotic aftermath, these men would have been more than grateful for the appearance of this YWCA canteen outside the Bush Hotel, High Street.

Acres and acres of the town had been laid waste by the bombings as this picture looking eastwards reveals.

Wartime Prime Minister Winston Churchill was not long in coming to Swansea to lift the morale of its brave people. Here he is pictured striding past the Bush Hotel, High Street, inspecting the damage, accompanied by his wife.

A roofless St Mary's Church stands amid the devastation.

Teilo Crescent, Mayhill, where some of the worst devastation of the German raids claimed 46 lives.

This is how the centre of Swansea looked in 1945 after most of the rubble and damaged buildings had been cleared away. An aerial view of Swansea in 1960 after much rebuilding work had been completed.

An aerial view of Swansea in 1960 after much rebuilding work had been completed.

Unforgettable Moments

A typical 1920s Swansea wedding.

Residents of Watkin Street, North Hill, celebrate the coronation of King George VI in 1937.

Youngsters of Ebenezer Street, wave their flags at the street party held to celebrate the coronation of King George VI.

It was a special day indeed for this young girl when she swapped her doll for a real baby in her toy pram, 1937.

Youngsters enjoy a Christmas party at the Elysium, High Street, late 1930s.

All dressed up for a special event at St Augustine's Church, Oakwood Road, Brynmill, late 1930s.

VE Day celebrations at Waun Wen Road, Waun Wen, 1945.

Residents of Milton Terrace, Mount Pleasant, on VE Day, 1945.

Young and old united at Ynysforgan to celebrate the end of World War Two, 1945.

VJ Day celebrations at Caedrawd Road, Mayhill, 1945.

All set for the carnival procession held at Ynysforgan to celebrate the end of World War Two, 1945.

Youngsters of Montpelier Terrace and Brooklands Terrace in fancy dress at their joint VE Day street party, 1945.

Neighbours of Hazel Road and Pinewood Avenue, Uplands, during their VE Day joint street party, 1945.

Residents of Hawthorne Avenue, Glanmor all dressed up top celebrate VJ Day, 1945.

A bride and groom from Mayhill, with the attendants at their 1940s wedding.

All smiles for the cameraman at this 1950s Swansea wedding.

Children of employees of the Elba Tinplate Works, Crymlyn Burrows, at their Christmas party, 1950.

Guests at a Morriston wedding, 1951.

Heol Emrys, Penlan, took to the street for its Festival of Britain party, May 1951.

Libanus Chapel, Morriston, was the scene of this 1951 wedding.

Employees of the Elba Tinplate Works, Crymlyn Burrows and their wives at the annual childrens' Christmas party, 1951.

A visit from Santa helped things along at this Christmas party for children at the orthopaedic clinic, Trinity House, Trinity Place, 1952.

Fun-filled faces at the Christmas party for children of employees at the Elba Works, 1952.

Chairs of all kinds helped in the seating arrangements when Rhoddfa'r Brain, Fforesthall, held its street party to celebrate the coronation of Queen Elizabeth II, June 1953.

A Christmas party at the YMCA for children of employees at the Viscose plant, 1963.

The coronation of Queen Elizabeth II was reason enough for these youngsters – including three members of the Huxtable family – at Rosehill Terrace, Mount Pleasant, to don fancy dress, June 1953.

A group of Landore residents celebrate the coronation of Queen Elizabeth II, June 1953.

Not so much a special day, more a special night in prospect as these three Sketty youngsters eye up an effigy of Guy Fawkes, November 5, 1954.

A wedding at St Gabriel's Church, Bryn Road, 1955.

The opening of a new Marks & Spencer store in Oxford Street was definitely a day to remember for these shoppers, December 1957.

Carmarthen Road Chapel, Waunwen was the scene of this 1961 wedding.

The flags flew high in Rodney Street, Sandfields, for celebrations to mark the Investiture of the Prince of Wales, July 1969.

Some of the residents of Carnglas Avenue, Tycoch who turned out in fancy dress to celebrate the silver jubilee of Queen Elizabeth II, July 1977.

Queen Elizabeth II is welcomed by guests as she arrives to perform the opening ceremony of Swansea Leisure Centre, 1977.

On Parade

New recruits and volunteers march off from the YMCA, along St Helen's Road, during World War One, 1914.

There was much commotion when this World War One tank rumbled through Swansea about 1920 to its eventual resting place at the Singleton Park end of St Helen's Recreation Ground. It was eventually taken away for scrap during World War Two.

Swansea Messenger Boys Band on the town's hospital carnival day, September 1, 1923.

A group of Swansea firemen, mid-1930s.

St John Ambulance Brigade cadets marching near the Guildhall, mid-1930s.

A detachment of Home Guard personnel pictured near the playing fields at Landore, early 1940s.

Some of the ICI Metals firemen with their appliance, 1940.

Inspection time for firemen at ICI Metals, Morfa Works, Landore, 1940.

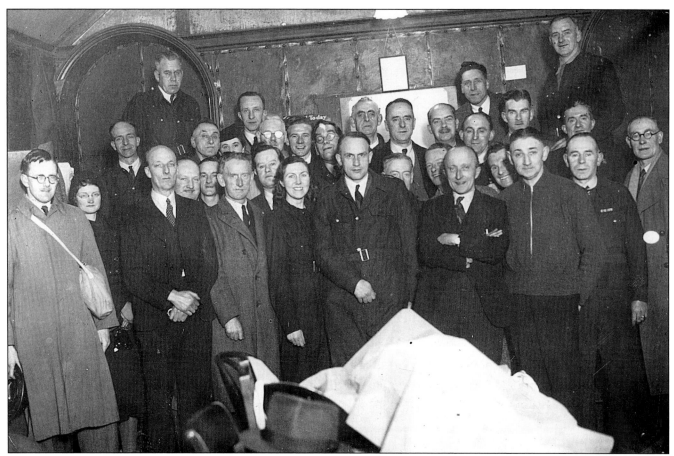

A group of World War Two air raid precaution volunteers in a basement room of their headquarters at Stewart Hall, Sketty, 1940.

Mount Pleasant and YWCA Guide troops combined to pack comfort parcels for troops during World War Two, 1940.

A Home Guard detachment, with band, awaits the arrival of a distinguished visitor to Swansea during World War Two, 1942.

Residents of Milton Terrace found themselves unexpectedly on parade when Queen Elizabeth, now the Queen Mother, visited war-damaged Swansea, 1941.

Another royal visitor, the Duke of Kent, chats to residents of Milton Terrace, 1941.

Scouts of the 25th St George troop all set to leave for their summer camp at Parkmill, Gower, 1945.

A detachment of women Home Guard volunteers, 1947. It was disbanded soon after.

Swansea Sea Cadets, 1959.

Swansea Sea Cadet band plays outside Swansea Museum, 1959.

Swansea Army Cadet Force, late 1970s.

The South Wales Police Band leads the Lord Mayor's Parade 1982.

District Diary

West Street, Gorseinon, mid-1890s. Then it was named Masons Road.

Southend, Mumbles, early 1900s.

Sketty Cross, early 1900s. This picture was taken from Vivian Road looking towards Broadway.

The bandstand at Victoria Park, early 1900s.

The railway crossing at Gorseinon, early 1900s. The footbridge can be seen behind the pony and trap.

The road from Gorseinon to Penllergaer, early 1900s.

An early 1900s panorama of Morriston. Tabernacle Chapel dominates the skyline.

Clyne Valley, 1905.

Uplands Crescent, during the snow of 1907. The picture shows that despite the snow the trams were still running.

St Martin's Church, Dunvant, a branch of Sketty Church, 1909. The site was later occupied by a filling station.

High Street, Gorseinon, 1911.

Swansea canal at Ynystawe, 1911.

Fforestfach and Cockett, about 1920.

A flooded Marlborough Road, Brynmill, September 11, 1930.

Sketty Green, 1930.

Needham's chemist store, 39 Neath Road, Hafod, 1925. Standing on the steps is popular Mr Needham, often referred to locally as the doctor.

Pentremawr Road, Hafod, 1931.

Looking over Sketty towards Mumbles, from Lon Coed Bran, 1935. The new housing foundations in the foreground meant that the view would soon be lost forever.

A South Wales Transport bus tackles the steep climb of Penygraig Road, early 1950s.

The war memorial and gardens, Morriston, early 1950s.

Eastmoor Nursery, Clyne Common, 1952.

The entrance to Morriston hospital, mid-1950s.

The Mumbles train picks up passengers at Brynmill, mid-1950s.

Pentrepoeth Road, Morriston, mid-1950s.

With the Mumbles Train at an end, buses ply their trade along Mumbles Road, early 1960s.

Clyne Court Flats, Sketty, in the snow of 1962.

Woodfield Street, Morriston, mid-1960s.

Pluck Lake, in the Lower Swansea Valley during the early days of the industrial reclamation scheme, 1968.

The road at Llangyfelach, 1968.

An aerial view of Llansamlet, 1972.

Martin Street School, Morriston, 1974.

Bonymaen adventure playground, 1975.

The site of the former Swansea Vale Smelting Works, now part of Swansea Enterprise Park, 1978.

Byron Crescent, Mayhill, after heavy snow, 1981.

A snow-blocked Carnglas Avenue, Sketty, 1981.

The Malvern Terrace, Brynmill, back lane made a great toboggan run for these children in the snow of 1981.

Woodfield Street, Morriston, 1982.

Early Learning

Class 6, Hafod School, 1912.

Standard 1, Terrace Road Girls' School, 1919.

Class 6 Brynmill Boys' School, 1913.

Pupils of Penclawdd Infants School, 1928.

Standard 1C, Brynhyfryd Infants School, 1929.

Pupils of Oxford Street School, late 1930s.

A class of juniors at Three Crosses School, 1935.

Class 4, Tirdeunaw Mixed School, 1937.

Boys of Plasmarl School, 1946.

Members of Morriston Congregational Chapel's Sunday School, winners of the Swansea Scripture Shield, 1950.

The Verse Chorus of Martin Street School, Morriston, 1951.

Boys from Oxford Street School at Victoria Park for sports lessons, 1951.

Children at Eastmoor Nursery, Clyne Common, 1952.

Students at Gregg School on a visit to St Fagan's Welsh Folk Museum, 1952.

Pupils of Gendros School, 1952.

Class J4, Gwyrosydd Primary School, 1953. Theirs was the first class at the new school to sit the 11-plus examination.

Dynevor Grammar School boys, late 1950s.

Children at Mayhill Junior School, 1954.

Children and staff at Eastmoor Nursery, on Bonfire Night, 1955.

Class 1B, Terrace Road Junior School, 1954.

A class at Cwm School, 1957.

Class J2 Terrace Road School, 1957.

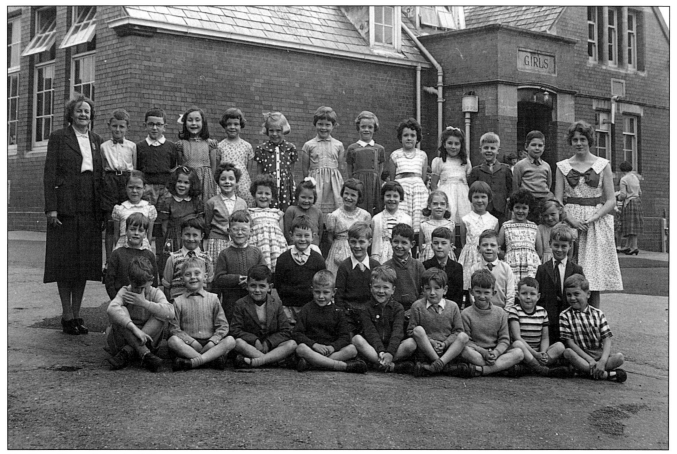

Pupils at Sketty School, 1959.

Some of the pupils of Form 5 North, Glanmor Grammar School for girls, 1959.

Class J4, Terrace Road School, 1959.

Pupils of Ynystawe Infants School, 1961.

Children of Terrace Road Sunday School, have a visit from Santa, Christmas 1962.

A class at Brynhyfryd Infants School, 1964.

Cwmbwrla Junior School, 1966.

Children at Ynystawe Junior School, 1966.

Mayhill Primary School pupils, early 1960s.

The reception class at Terrace Road School, April 1967.

A class at Brynmill Infants School, 1969.

Penllergaer Nursery School children, 1970.

Class J3, Brynmill Primary School, 1971.

Class 1, Terrace Road Infants School, 1971.

Class 1, Terrace Road Junior School, 1971.

Class J4, Brynmill Primary School, 1974.

Boys and girls of Oxford Street School, 1975.

Class 4P, Morriston Primary School, 1979.

Pupils at Ffynone House School, 1985.

A class at Ffynone House School, 1985.

Pupils of Terrace Road School, during centenary celebrations, 1985.

Senior pupils at Ffynone House School, 1988.

Beside The Seaside

Mumbles village, early 1900s.

Langland Bay, 1908.

The west pier at Swansea Beach, 1911.

Fern Bank Cabin was a holiday home – 1912 style – at Langland. Later the site became known as Higher Lane.

Caswell Bay, 1913. The windmill once used to pump water can clearly be seen on the headland.

A summer camp in fields above Langland Bay, 1920.

A family get together at Langland, 1922.

Mumbles Pier, 1923.

The new road linking Mumbles with Bracelet Bay and Limeslade, 1933.

A Swansea family on holiday in a Gower chalet, 1933.

The sands at Crymlyn Burrows was a haven for these youngsters in 1936.

There was sand and the sea, so the oil tanks really didn't matter at Crymlyn Burrows, for this young girl and her dog, 1937.

A family day on the beach at Crymlyn Burrows, 1937.

Limeslade, 1949.

A family day out, near Three Cliffs Bay, Gower, 1949.

Mumbles pier and lighthouse, early 1950s.

On the beach at Porteynon, early 1950s.

The foreshore at Southend, early 1950s.

Mumbles Pier café and the Mumbles train viewed from the pier, mid-1950s.

Roundabout fun on the sands at the Slip, 1955.

Boating fun at Oxwich, Gower, early 1960s.

On the pebbles at Bracelet Bay, early 1960s.

On the foreshore at Blackpill, August 1961.

Worm's Head, Rhossili, Gower, 1972.

A sheltered cove at Caswell, July, 1975.

Looking towards Mumbles Head from Limes lade, 1975.

Moving Memories

The North Dock basin, August 6, 1904.

HMS Robin, a shallow-draft gunship, at Swansea Docks, 1904.

A practice launch for the Mumbles Lifeboat, at Southend, July 1905.

Full up! The Mumbles train prepares to return hundreds of day-trippers to Swansea and beyond, 1906.

This group is all set for a charabanc outing, March 1908. The picture was taken outside Swansea baths and laundry, St Helen's Road.

Commercial traveller for United Breweries, James Davies, went about his rounds in this pony and cart, 1908.

Sunday was the day for a stroll down to the promenade, in 1912 – or perhaps a ride on the Mumbles train.

Sailing vessels alongside more modern, steam-powered ships, in North Dock, 1912.

The Mumbles train passes St Helen's, 1914.

The Prince of Wales travelled in style when he visited Swansea and Mumbles on June 27, 1919.

This GWK make car, owned by a Swansea family is pictured in a lane at Langland, 1922.

One of the six-wheel steam wagons operated by Gorseinon haulier Gwynne Bowen, late 1920s.

This was how removal company W. Laugharne Morgan carried their loads in 1929.

A steam wagon operated by Edward Jenkins & Son, Landore, outside their garage at Brynhyfryd Square, early 1930s.

This coach, outside Cross Buildings, Morriston, was owned by E. Harris & Sons bus company, late 1930s.

A Pickfords removal van negotiates a narrow lane in the Swansea Valley, mid-1930s.

King's Dock, 1932.

A British Road Services crew with their lorry and its trailer, at Brynhyfryd Square, late 1940s.

Swan Bus company double deckers parked near Plymouth Street, 1950.

The oil tanker Atlantic Duchess lies in the Queen's dock, her back broken by a huge explosion, February 1951.

A woman driver makes some last-minute adjustments to her car before taking part in a mid-1950s rally.

Single deck, AEC Regent buses like this, operated by the South Wales Transport company, were a familiar sight during the 1950s. This one is pictured travelling along Harbour Road.

Unloading tea at the King's Dock, mid-1950s.

Chaos at Blackpill following a collision between two Mumbles trains, 1956.

Steam and diesel power in evidence at High Street railway station, 1958.

The fleet's in! Coaches that is. Morris Bros. lined up their vehicles for the cameraman at Bracelet Bay, early 1960s.

Locomotive Cadbury Castle on the Landore loop to Cockett with the West Wales portion of the 8.55am Paddington to Pembroke Dock train on February 3, 1959.

Work begins on dismantling the Mumbles Railway's famous tramcars just days after the service ended in January 1960.

A train leaves Swansea Victoria station bound for Shrewsbury, early 1960s.

One of South Wales Transport's experimental, unpainted, silver AEC Regent double decker buses, at Caer Street, mid-1960s.

A train prepares to leave Victoria Station for Pontarddulais, on June 6, 1964.

Working Wonders

Residents of Swansea Workhouse, Mount Pleasant, late 1890s.

Sketty blacksmith George Blundell, early 1900s.

Cobbler and boot repairer A. Townsend, surrounded by rolls of leather, outside his Cockett workshop, early 1900s.

Men and women farm workers at Caereithin, 1904.

Swansea women who worked at Pembrey munitions factory, 1914.

Swansea munitions factory workers, 1916.

The boilerman at Morriston Star Laundry, 1920.

H. Poley and Sons' fishmongery, Wind Street, April 1922.

A salvage crew at Swansea Docks, late 1920s.

This horse-drawn dust cart was a familiar sight in early 1930s Swansea.

Construction workers employed on the Mumbles sewer scheme, 1935.

Counter staff at John Hall Tools, Gower Street, 1935.

Employees of the Upper Forest and Worcester Tinplate Works, Morriston, late 1940s.

Young tinplate workers at the Elba Works, 1950.

Bottling pickles at the ET Pickle factory, Hafod, 1950. The ET stood for Emmanuel Thomas. They bottled mineral water as well.

Swansea members of the Painters and Decorators Guild of Great Britain enjoy a little laughter at their annual dinner, 1950s.

Council workers in Townhill, 1950s.

An early 1950s industrial panorama, showing the Dyffryn Works at Morriston.

Women workers at Baths Laundry, 1955.

Workers at Tir John power station, Port Tennant, late 1950s.

The chipping bay at Dyffryn Tinplate Works, Morriston, 1959.

Swansea dockers take a break in their canteen, 1960.

Workmates of Metal Box and Corker & Bevan celebrate Christmas, 1960.

Shipwrights at Palmer's Dry Dock, Swansea, 1960.

Staff of Burtons, College Street forsake selling gents clothing to help clear the pavement outside of snow, 1962.

The foundry of Metalclad, Morriston, part of the Cohen group, May 1964.

Staff of Morsmith Motors, Carmarthen Road, gather to say farewell to a colleague, early 1960s.

A busy time for staff at the Nelson Street Walkaround Store, late 1960s.

Canteen staff at Townhill School, 1961.

Celebration time for these workers at the Addis factory, Pentrechwyth, late 1960s.

Workers at the Signode strapping plant, Fforestfach, 1967.

An unusual job for these council workers – laying the crazy golf course near Singleton Park's boating lake.

Penclawdd milkman Gwyn Harry and a young helper. Gwyn was still delivering by horse and cart in 1972.

Production line staff at sponge manufacturers Spontex, at South Dock, 1972.

Jean Harris shows Swansea East MP Neil McBride and Neath MP Donald Coleman some of the workings of the Driver and Vehicle Licensing Centre, Clase, Morriston, 1972.

Viscose factory staff, late 1970s.

Team Spirit

Llangyfelach Harriers Hunt, 1904.

Sketty Association Football Club, 1908-09.

Danycoed Cricket Club, Morriston, 1912.

Swansea Ladies AFC, 1918.

Swansea University Hockey Team, 1924.

Members of Swansea Amateur Fencing Club, with a civic visitor, 1946.

Brynmill Boys Junior School football squad, 1948-49.

Members of Elba Tinplate Works rugby squad, 1946-47.

Cadle Junior School football squad, 1948.

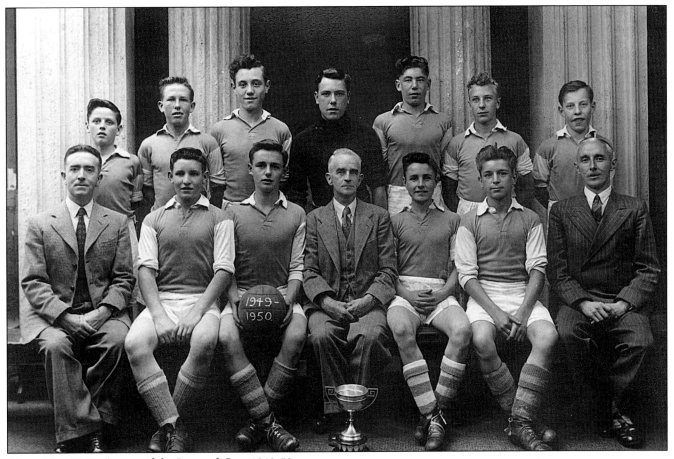

Waun Wen AFC, winners of the Leonard Cup, 1949-50.

Waun Wen Junior School football team, 1949.

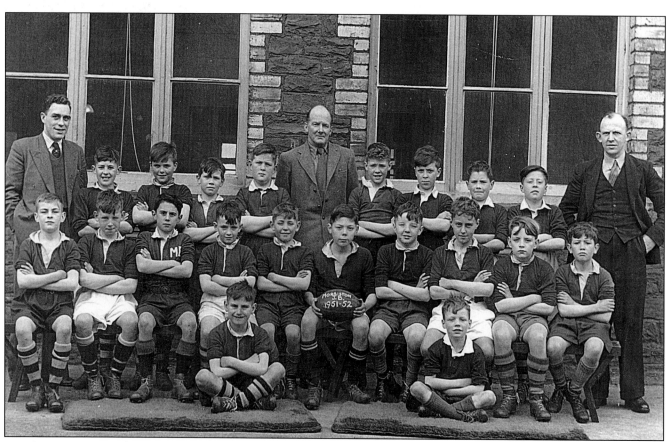

Martin Street Junior School rugby squad, 1951.

Elba Works rugby side in action, in the dark shirts, 1951.

The Gregg School football team, 1952.

Morriston Junior School rugby squad, 1953.

The Star Inn, Fforestfach, football team, mid-1950s.

Penlan Comprehensive School football team, 1958.

Portmead Junior School football squad, 1960.

Dynevor School football team, 1961.

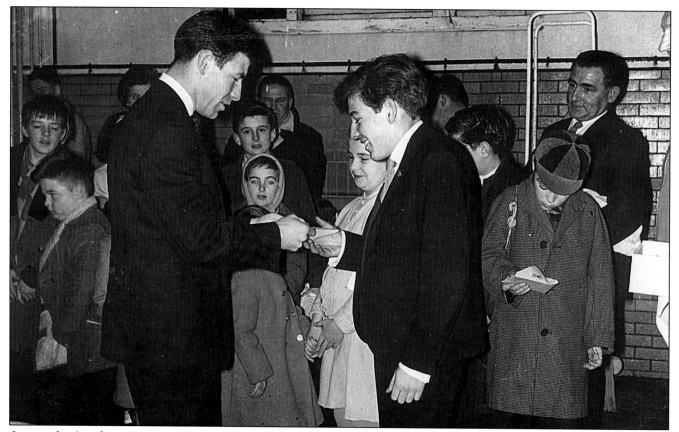

Swansea boxing champion Brian Curvis presents Red Cross swimming awards to a group of youngsters, early 1960s.

Bishop Gore School swimming team, 1967.

Woodman Rangers football squad, 1967.

Penlan Comprehensive School senior football squad, 1967.

Ravenhill bowls team, 1968.

Olchfa School basketball team, 1970.

Emmanuel Grammar School Old Boys rugby squad, 1972.

Bishop Gore Comprehensive School hockey squad, early 1970s.

Swansea Otters Swimming Club 1975.

Morriston Boys Junior School football squad, 1980. They won the Swansea Schools' Football Association Cup Final at Vetch Field and were also Swansea Schools' League Champions.